Rocks and Fossils

KINGFISHER

Published in 2011 by Kingfisher
This edition published in 2013 by Kingfisher
an imprint of Macmillan Children's Books
a division of Macmillan Publishers Limited
20 New Wharf Road, London N1 9RR
Basingstoke and Oxford
Associated companies throughout the world
www.panmacmillan.com

ISBN 978-0-7534-3729-2

First published as *Kingfisher Young Knowledge: Rocks and Fossils* in 2003
Additional material produced for Macmillan Children's Books by Discovery Books Ltd

Copyright © Macmillan Children's Books 2011

1 3 5 7 9 8 6 4 2
1SPL/0713/WKT/UTD/128MA

A CIP catalogue record for this book is available from the British Library.

Printed in China

Note to readers: the website addresses listed in this book are correct at the time of going to print.
However, due to the ever-changing nature of the internet, website addresses and content can
change. Websites can contain links that are unsuitable for children. The publisher cannot be held
responsible for changes in website addresses or content, or for information obtained through
a third party. We strongly advise that internet searches be supervised by an adult.

Acknowledgements

The publisher would like to thank the following for permission to reproduce their material. Every care has been taken
to trace copyright holders. However, if there have been unintentional omissions or failure to trace copyright holders,
we apologise and will, if informed, endeavour to make corrections in any future edition.
b = bottom, *c* = centre, *l* = left, *t* = top, *r* = right

cover Shutterstock/Sergio Gutierrez Getino; Shutterstock/ChinellatoPhoto; Shutterstock/Mirka Moksha;
Shutterstock/Tyler Olson; Shutterstock/kojihirano; *pages* 1 Corbis; 2–3 Corbis; 4–5 Geoscience Features;
6–7 Corbis; 7*br* C. & H. S. Pellant; 8–9 Corbis; 9*tr* G. Brad Lewis/Science Photo Library; 10–11 (sky)
Dynamic Graphic; 10*tr* C. & H. S. Pellant; 10*bl* Corbis; 11 Corbis; 12–13 Geoscience Features;
12*cl* C. & H. S. Pellant; 13*cl* C. & H. S. Pellant; 14–15 Corbis; 15*tl* C. & H. S. Pellant; 15*cr* Science Photo
Library; 16*cl* C. & H. S. Pellant; 16–17 Corbis; 17*tl* Geoscience Features; 18–19 Corbis; 19*tl* Frank Lane
Picture Library; 19*cr* Frank Lane Picture Library; 20–21 (sky) Dynamic Graphic; 20–21 (rock) Science Photo
Library; 21*tr* Corbis; 21*br* Corbis; 22–23 Corbis; 22*tl* Science Photo Library; 23*tr* Corbis; 24–25 Science
Photo Library; 25*tl* Digital Science; 25*br* Corbis; 26–27 Corbis; 26*bl* Corbis; 27*l* Corbis; 28–29 Corbis;
28*bl* David M. Dennis/Oxford Scientific Films; 29*tl* Corbis; 30–31 Corbis; 30*b* Science Photo Library;
31*c* Corbis; 32–33 Corbis; 32*bl* Corbis; 33*b* Corbis; 34–35 Corbis; 34*br* Ardea; 35*tl* Science Photo Library;
35*r* Corbis; 36–37 Michael Fogden/Oxford Scientific Films; 37*t* Science Photo Library; 37*cr* Geoscience
Features; 38–39 Corbis; 39*tr* Corbis; 39*cl* Science Photo Library; 40–41 David M. Dennis/Oxford Scientific
Films; 40*b* Science Photo Library; 41*cr* Science Photo Library; 42–43 Geoscience Features; 42*bl* Corbis;
43*tr* Corbis; 45*tr* Geoscience Features; 46*tr* Corbis; 48 iStockphoto/Josef Friedhuber; 49*t* Shutterstock
Images/markrhiggins; 49*b* Shutterstock Images/alexia; 52*t* Shutterstock Images/dinadesign;
52*b* Wikimedia/Meckimac; 53*t* Shutterstock Images/Ziga Camernik; 53*b* iStockphoto/Kun Jiang;
56 Shutterstock Images/Roger De Marfa

Commissioned photography on pages 44–45 by Geoff Dann; 46–47 by Andy Crawford
Thank you to models Daniel Newton and Eleanor Davis

Rocks and Fossils

Chris Pellant

KINGFISHER

Contents

What is a rock?   6

Rocks from heat   8

Rough and smooth   10

Second-hand rocks   12

Layer by layer   14

Rocks that change   16

Under pressure   18

Wear and tear   20

Rain, roots and ice   22

Rocks from space   24

The uses of rocks   26

What is a fossil?   28

How fossils form   30

Ancient sea creatures   32

34 The age of dinosaurs

36 Fossil plants

38 Fossil fuels

40 Clues from fossils

42 How to find fossils

44 Project: Fun with fossils

46 Project: Rocks around you

48 Glossary

50 Parent and teacher notes

52 Did you know?

54 Rocks and fossils quiz

55 Find out more

56 Index

What is a rock?

The Earth's crust is made of rocks. Some rocks are hard and solid, such as granite. Others are soft, such as sand. All rocks are made of minerals.

Craggy landscape

Here, in the Sierra Nevada mountains, USA, weather has damaged a granite mountain top and broken it into large, rounded boulders.

Grains of granite

Granite is made of different coloured
minerals. The pink mineral is called
feldspar, the grey one is quartz and
the black one is called mica.

7

8 Rocks from heat

Deep under the Earth's crust, the rock is so hot it is liquid. This molten rock is called magma. Sometimes the magma breaks through weak spots in the crust and reaches the surface. This is what happens when a volcano erupts.

Cooling lava

When the red-hot magma reaches the surface it is called lava. Lava takes a long time to cool.

Igneous rocks

As the lava cools it hardens and becomes rock. We call rocks that are made in this way, from heat, igneous rocks.

Rough and smooth

As molten rock cools, crystals are formed from the minerals. Large crystals grow if the rock cools slowly. Small crystals grow if the rock cools quickly.

Medium crystals
This microgranite rock has smaller crystals than granite because it cooled more quickly.

Lava columns
Basalt has tiny crystals and can have a smooth surface. It often cools into six-sided columns.

Cracks for climbing

Granite has large crystals. When granite magma cools, cracks form in the rock. Climbers grip the cracks as they climb.

Second-hand rocks

Sand, mud and pebbles in a river or lake, or on the seabed, can be turned into rocks called sedimentary rocks. These can be told apart from others because they have layers, or strata.

Shell rock
Limestone is often made of tiny shells. Curved snail shells can be seen in this rock.

sea-cliff

Sandy cliffs

These cliffs in Dorset, UK, are made of layers of sand that settled on the seabed millions of years ago. They have been tightly pressed together to form layers of rock.

Layer by layer

There are three different types of sedimentary rocks. One type is made of the remains of dead sea animals. Another is made of mud, sand or pebbles. The third is made when water evaporates.

Tiny creatures

Limestone is made of the skeletons of millions of tiny sea creatures. It is worn away, or weathered, easily, often forming scenery like this.

Rock gypsum

Seawater contains minerals. When it evaporates, minerals stay behind and form rocks, such as this gypsum.

Made of sand

Sandstone is a very common rock. It often forms colourful layers, such as those you can see in this picture.

Rocks that change

Rocks change when they are heated deep underground – their crystals grow larger. Limestone, a sedimentary rock, turns into a metamorphic rock called marble. Layers in the rock disappear as it takes on a new form.

Fossil layers

Limestone is a rock formed in the sea and contains fossils. These fossils break down when the rock changes into marble.

Smooth marble

Marble has millions of pale crystals made of a mineral called calcite, stuck together tightly like a jigsaw.

Monumental rock

Marble is cut into many different shapes, and used for ornaments, sculptures and gravestones.

Under pressure

As the Earth's crust moves, any rocks deep down are twisted and squashed, and their shape is changed by pressure.

Twisted gneiss

Gneiss rock has twisted bands of dark and pale minerals. It used to be granite, and is formed by the greatest pressure.

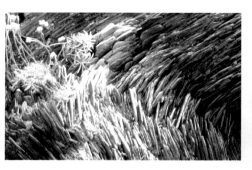

Slivers of slate

Slate is made when the pressure underground is not very great. This rock breaks into thin slabs and can be used for roof tiles.

Silvery schist

Schist is formed in mountainous areas by medium pressure. Its silvery surface is covered with the mineral mica.

Wear and tear

Rocks do not last for ever. They are battered by the sea on the coasts. High in the mountains, glaciers grind rocks to dust. Rivers carve valleys into the land.

Sandblasted

This arch is all that is left of a huge cliff. Sand carried in the wind blows against it constantly and wears it away.

Deep cuts

Rocks, sand and pebbles carried in rivers pound against the river banks, and can cut deep gorges into the land.

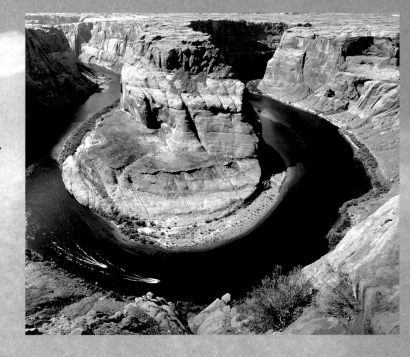

Wave power

Waves hurl rocks and stones at the cliffs, slowly breaking down the coastline.

Rain, roots and ice

Growing roots
Plants grow in cracks in rocks. As their roots grow, they push the cracks further apart.

Rocks are damaged by the weather. They shrink in the cold and expand when it is hot. Rainwater gets into cracks. When the water freezes, the ice expands the cracks and the rock shatters.

Ice-breaking

This mountain ridge shows how ice can break rocks apart to form jagged points.

Washed away

This rock is a strange shape because rainwater has weathered it over many years.

Rocks from space

There are many rocks in space, of different shapes and sizes. They are called meteorites and are rocks left over from when the planets formed. Sometimes, meteorites crash down to Earth.

Impact crater

This huge crater in Arizona, USA, was formed when a gigantic meteorite smashed into Earth. It is over a kilometre across – more than the length of 14 jumbo jets.

Explosive rock

When large meteorites hit the ground, they explode. The heat from the explosion melts the rocks around them, making glassy stones called tektites.

Hot metal

Most meteorites are made of metal, like this one. As they rush through the sky, they become extremely hot and can be seen as trails of light.

The uses of rocks

Rocks are used in thousands of ways.
Without rocks, there would be no
bricks, cement, glass or coal. Most
industry is based on
the use of rocks.

Potty about clay
Clay is an
important rock.
As well as being
used for pottery,
it is used to make
cement and even
washing powder.

Angelic rock

Pale marble is a favourite rock for carving into statues, such as this angel.

Carved in stone

Many of the world's finest buildings are made from cut rock. Sedimentary rocks can be cut into neat blocks for building, and all rocks can be carved into delicate shapes.

What is a fossil?

Any trace of a plant or animal that lived in the past is a fossil, such as a shell preserved in rock layers for millions of years. The black outlines of delicate ferns and the massive footprints of dinosaurs are also fossils.

Trilobite
This creature lived in the sea hundreds of millions of years ago. Its modern relatives include insects, crabs and spiders.

Big bones

These dinosaur bones were uncovered in the Dinosaur National Monument, Colorado, USA.

Uncovering the past

A fossil expert, or palaeontologist, works very carefully to expose part of a huge dinosaur skeleton at the Dinosaur National Monument.

How fossils form

Dead creatures and plants may
be buried in sand or mud. This
is when fossilization begins.
The soft parts of the animal
rot away, while the hard
parts – its shell or bones –
become fossilized.

Stuck fast, forever
This ant is caught in
the sticky resin oozing
from a tree. It will die
there and may
become a fossil.

Fossilized fly

Millions of years ago, this fly became trapped in resin, which hardened to amber, fossilizing the fly.

Ammonites

Ammonites swam in the sea when dinosaurs roamed the land. They are close relatives of squids and octopuses.

ammonite

Ancient sea creatures

Fossils of dead sea creatures lie buried under the constant build-up of muddy and sandy layers on the seabed. Trilobites, corals, molluscs and starfish are all common fossils from the ancient seas.

Tropical fossils

Corals build their homes out of limestone, often in tropical seas. Fossil corals tell geologists where these seas were long ago.

fossilized fish

Stone starfish

Even delicate animals such as this starfish can be fossilized. This fossil has formed in shale – a sedimentary rock formed on the seabed from packed mud.

The age of dinosaurs

Nobody has ever seen a dinosaur because they became extinct millions of years ago. We only know about dinosaurs from finding fossils of their bones, footprints and eggs.

dinosaur fossil footprint

Buried in rock

This Stegosaurus fossil was found buried in Wyoming, in the USA. It clearly shows the shape of the dinosaur.

Dinosaur eggs

Dinosaurs laid
eggs, just like
birds do today.
We can find
fossils of baby
dinosaurs in eggs
such as these.

Stegosaurus

Scientists built
this Stegosaurus
skeleton from fossil
bones like those
in the picture
on the left.

Fossil plants

Fossils of stems and tree trunks are common, especially in rocks that contain seams of coal. Among the seams, even fossils of delicate ferns may be found.

Stone trees
These trees were changed by fossilization – they are now made of a mineral called silica, instead of wood.

From old...

Delicate, beautiful fern leaves are fossilized as thin layers of carbon between the layers of rock.

...to modern

A modern fern is just like fossil ferns hundreds of millions of years old.

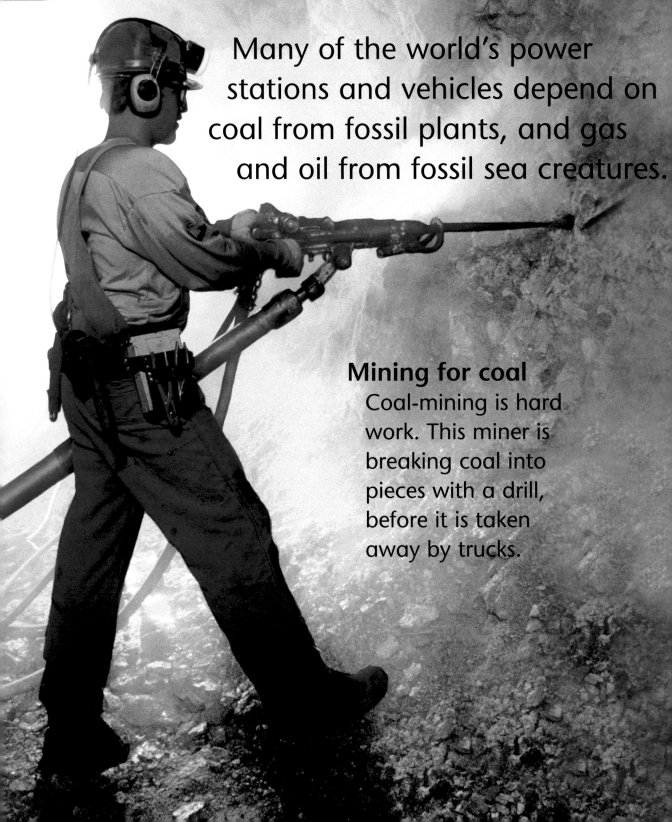

Fossil **fuels**

Many of the world's power
stations and vehicles depend on
coal from fossil plants, and gas
and oil from fossil sea creatures.

Mining for coal
Coal-mining is hard
work. This miner is
breaking coal into
pieces with a drill,
before it is taken
away by trucks.

Fossils for driving

Oil is a fossil fuel from which many products, including petrol and diesel oil, are made.

Poisonous fuel

Coal is a black, shiny rock. It has been used as a fuel for hundreds of years. However, when it is burned, poisonous smoke billows out and causes much pollution.

Clues from fossils

Fossils tell us about life millions of years ago. Scientists can reconstruct the bodies of extinct creatures and study how animals and plants have evolved.

Alive and well

The coelacanth fish was known only as a fossil. Then, in 1938, living coelacanths were caught off the South African coast.

These footprints, made in soft mud over three million years ago, show that our ancestors walked upright at that time.

archaeopteryx

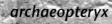

Archaeopteryx

This is one of the most famous fossils. The skeleton looks like a small dinosaur, but there are impressions of feathers. Experts believe that modern birds are descended from dinosaurs.

How to find fossils

Fossils can be found near cliffs or quarries, or in other areas that have sedimentary rock. However, these can be dangerous places, and you must never visit them without an adult.

Cliff-hanger
Palaeontologists go to many different places to search for fossils and it can be dangerous work. This fossil-hunter is carefully unearthing fossils on a steep slope.

Beach treasure

Fossils may fall from cliffs and land on the beaches below. Be careful around cliffs and beware of falling rocks.

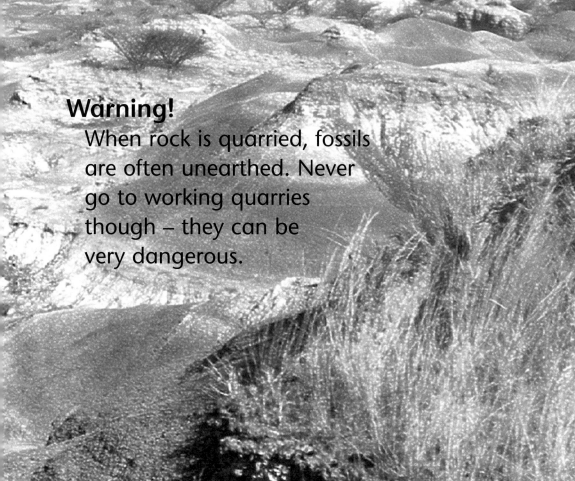

Warning!

When rock is quarried, fossils are often unearthed. Never go to working quarries though – they can be very dangerous.

Fun with fossils

You will need
- 5 balls of coloured dough
- Shells

Roll the dough into flat cakes. Sprinkle the first cake with shells. These will be your fossils.

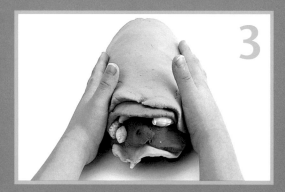

Push the sides together to make an arch. This happens when rocks are squeezed together.

Making mountains
Layers of rock can be squashed together and forced up to make mountains. Any fossils in the layers then come to the surface.

Add two more layers of dough and shells. Then put two layers of dough on top. Do not put any shells in the top two layers.

Ask an adult to slice off the top. The first layers put down are now in the middle. They are the oldest layers and have the oldest fossils.

Amazing ammonites

Make your own fossil with modelling clay and moulding plaster. Use a real fossil or a shell to make a cast.

You will need
- Modelling clay
- Fossil or shell
- Moulding plaster
- Cup and spoon
- Paint
- Paintbrush

1

Roll some modelling clay into a ball. Press your fossil or shell, patterned side down, into the clay to make the cast.

2

Mix some moulding plaster with water in a cup and carefully spoon or pour it into the cast. Leave to set.

3

Once your fossil has set hard, carefully lift it from the cast. You may be able to use the cast again to make more fossils.

4

Your fossil is now ready to paint. Use any colours you like. Copy the colours of the shell or fossil, or paint it in brighter colours.

Rock collection

When you start rock collecting, label your rocks and record where you found them to organize your collection.

An eggbox is an ideal place for your collection. Use a different box for different types or colours of rock. Paint your eggbox.

You will need
- Eggbox
- Paint
- Paintbrush
- Cup for holding water
- Magnifying glass
- Sticky labels
- Notepad
- Pen

Examine the rock using a magnifying glass. You may be able to see the different coloured minerals that form the rock.

Number all your rocks, starting from 1. Write the number of the rock on a sticky label and stick it onto the rock.

In your notepad, write the number, where and when you found the rock, and the rock type. If you do not know the type, leave a space to fill it in later.

Finally, once the paint on your eggbox has dried, put your rock into it making sure the label can be seen. Congratulations! You have begun your rock collection.

How are rocks used?

Rocks are used in many ways. Look around you at home and outside, and draw the rocks that you see.

You will need
- Notepad
- Pen

You may see rocks as part of a wall, pavement or building. How many different uses of rocks can you find?

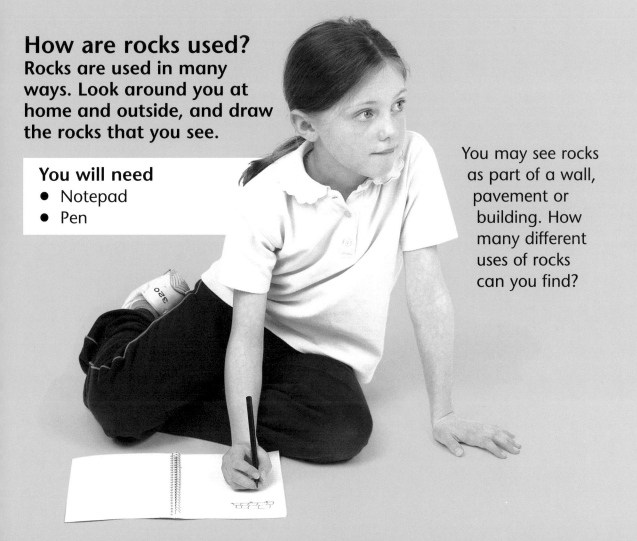

Glossary

Carbon – a chemical found in coal, diamonds and graphite

Cement – a clay-limestone mixture that is used to make concrete

Column – a tall, narrow pillar

Crater – a hole in the ground made by a meteorite or a volcanic explosion

Crust – the Earth's outermost layer, some of which lies under oceans

Crystal – a hard, glassy-looking object made of minerals

Evaporate – when a liquid changes into a gas

Evolved – to have changed gradually over time

Expand – to get bigger

Explode – to blow up, usually with a loud bang

Extinct – when an animal or plant species has completely died out

Fossil – the remains of a living thing from the past preserved in rock

Fuel – a substance that can be burned to produce heat or power

Glacier – a large, slow-moving mass of ice

Gorge – a steep-sided valley carved into the land by a river

Lava – molten rock on Earth's surface

Magma – molten rock when it is underground

Metamorphic – a change of form, usually by heat or pressure

Mineral – one of the natural substances that make up different rocks

Mollusc – a soft-bodied animal, such as a clam or a slug

Mountainous – describes a high area of mountains

Palaeontologist – someone who studies fossils

Pollution – chemicals, gases and other materials that damage the environment

Preserved – kept in good condition

Pressure – when a weight is pressing down on something

Quarry – a place from which stone is cut

Reconstruct – rebuilding to show how something once looked

Resin – the sticky sap that oozes from pine trees

Seabed – the bottom of the sea

Seam – a thin layer of a substance, such as coal

Skeleton – the frame of bones inside an animal's body

Strata – layers of rock

Weathered – damaged or broken down by wind, water or ice

Parent and teacher notes

This book includes material that would be particularly useful in helping to teach children aged 7–11. It covers many elements of the English and Science curricula (especially how the Earth is formed) and some cross-curricular lessons involving geography (how continents, mountains and rivers are shaped) and history.

Extension activities

Reading
Find out about Mary Anning, who collected fossils in Victorian times. Her life story will tell you a lot about fossils and also about life in the 19th century.

Writing
Find six different uses of rocks and minerals in this book. Present the information in a table or as a report.

Read about dinosaurs on pages 34–35. Imagine you have travelled in time to spend a day with them. Write a story about how you would survive.

Research four dinosaurs and write a report comparing their strengths and weaknesses. Which would win in a fight between them?

Speaking and listening
Imagine you are a radio reporter watching a meteorite crash into the Earth (see pages 24–25). Describe what you see as it falls and lands to form a crater.

Make a two-minute presentation explaining the good and bad things about coal (see pages 38–39).

Science
Imagine you are building a house. What different rocks would you use for the floors, walls and roof?

Read how rocks change when heated (page 16). What other materials do this? Which do not?

Page 22 shows how frozen water breaks rocks. Fill a small plastic container with water and put it in the freezer. What happens when the water freezes?

Go on a local hunt for different footprints left in mud (see page 41). How many different animal and other prints can you find?

Ask an adult to take you on a hunt for rocks and/or fossils. How many different rocks can you find? What do the fossils tell you?

Cross-curricular links
Geography: Pages 18–19 show how the Earth's crust moves. Photocopy a map of the world and cut out the continents. They were once joined. Can you fit them together like the pieces of a jigsaw?

Pages 20–21 show the effects of erosion. What features in your local area have been shaped by erosion?

Art and design: Create a rocky landscape using chicken wire and mod rock or moulding plaster.

Pages 10–11 describe rough and smooth rocks. Use different materials to make a textile collage with layers of a rocky landscape with rough and smooth textures.

Fossils show the shape of skeletons. Make your own animal skeletons using straws, or dried pasta. What would the animal have looked like when it was alive?

Make a leaf print picture to look like a collection of fossilised plants (see pages 36–37).

Using the projects
Children can follow or adapt these projects at home. Here are some ideas for extending them:

Page 44: Make a working model of a volcano with food colouring or paint for the lava. It can be made to erupt by adding vinegar to a small container of bicarbonate of soda hidden inside (also relates to pages 8–9).

Page 45: Try to copy an ammonite from a picture or real life.

Page 46: Choose the best materials to sketch each rock. Make a book about your collection.

Did you know?

- Diamonds are the hardest natural substance found on Earth.

- The most common rock on Earth is called basalt.

- There are over 900 different types of igneous rock.

- Almost 90 per cent of the Earth's upper crust is made out of igneous rock.

- The largest live volcano on Earth is Mauna Loa in Hawaii. It has been erupting on and off for at least 700,000 years!

- The largest ammonite fossils are often over 50 centimetres in diameter.

- The Taj Mahal in India is made entirely out of marble.

- The Great Pyramid of Giza in Egypt is made entirely of limestone.

- There are 1,500 active volcanoes around the world. At least 80 of these are found beneath the oceans.

- The longest dinosaur was called Seismosaurus. It measured over 40 metres long – that is as long as five double-decker buses.

- Globally, more electricity is produced by coal than any other energy source.

- The largest meteorite crater on Earth is called the Vredefort crater. It is in South Africa and measures 300 kilometres in diameter.

- The oldest known fossil is 3.5 million years old.

- There are over 3,000 different minerals in the world.

- The word *fossil* comes from the Latin word *fossilis*, which means 'dug up'.

Rocks and fossils quiz

The answers to these questions can all be found by looking back through the book. See how many you get right. You can check your answers on page 56.

1) What does igneous mean?
   A – Made from water
   B – Made from sand
   C – Made from fire

2) What is someone who hunts for fossils called?
   A – Biologist
   B – Palaeontologist
   C – Zoologist

3) What is molten rock called?
   A – Marble
   B – Magma
   C – Glacier

4) What sort of rock can fossils usually be found in?
   A – Sedimentary
   B – Igneous
   C – Metamorphic

5) What are the layers that make up sedimentary rocks called?
   A – Stacks
   B – Lines
   C – Strata

6) What is the mineral that makes up marble called?
   A – Calcite
   B – Brassite
   C – Tantite

7) What is limestone made from?
   A – Worms
   B – Gravel
   C – Skeletons of tiny sea creatures

8) How many types of sedimentary rock are there?
   A – 30
   B – 3
   C – 13

9) What are fossilized trees made out of?
   A – Silica
   B – Wood
   C – Sand

10) Where is schist formed?
    A – Mountainous areas
    B – Lowland areas
    C – Desert areas

11) Which of these rocks is formed when water evaporates?
    A – Limestone
    B – Gypsum
    C – Marble

12) What are rocks that have fallen from space called?
    A – Meteorites
    B – Stalagmites
    C – Kilobytes

Books to read

Basher: Rocks and Minerals by Simon Basher and Dan Green, Kingfisher, 2010

Geology Rocks! Fossils by Rebecca Faulkner, Raintree Publishers, 2008

Rocks and Minerals (Eyewitness Project Books), Dorling Kindersley, 2008

Rocks and Minerals (Scholastic True or False) by Melvin Berger, Scholastic Paperbacks, 2010

100 Facts on Rocks and Minerals by Sean Callery, Miles Kelly Publishing Ltd, 2009

100 Rocks and Minerals (Usborne Spotter's Cards) by Philip Clarke, Usborne Publishing Ltd, 2008

Places to visit

Cheddar Caves & Gorge
www.cheddarcaves.co.uk
Cheddar gorge in Somerset is the perfect example of a limestone gorge. Visitors to the gorge can investigate caves, enjoy an open-top bus tour and explore the museum.

Wookey Hole
www.wookey.co.uk
Wookey Hole caves are some of the most impressive in the United Kingdom.

Dolaucothi Gold Mines
www.nationaltrust.org.uk/dolaucothi-gold-mines
At the Dolaucothi Gold Mines you can explore the mines, see and hear 1930s mining equipment and even pan for gold yourself.

The Natural History Museum
www.nhm.ac.uk
Natural History Museum in London has a vast selection of fossils on display, ranging from huge full-skeleton dinosaurs to trilobites.

Websites

BBC – Science and Nature: Prehistoric Life
www.bbc.co.uk/nature/fossils
This website contains many videos of amazing fossil finds and what they can tell us about prehistoric life.

National Geographic: Earth
http://science.nationalgeographic.com/science/earth.html
The National Geographic website has information about how rocks are formed, the debate over the use of fossil fuels and some amazing videos of natural occurences from around the world.

Oxford University Museum of Natural History: The Learning Zone
www.oum.ox.ac.uk/thezone/rocks/index.htm
This website has facts about both rocks and fossils. There are also a number of activities and games, including a quiz.

amber 31
ammonites 31, 52
archaeopteryx 41
basalt 10, 52
carving 17, 27
clay 26
cliffs 13, 21, 42–43
coal 36, 38, 39, 53
coelacanths 40
corals 32
crystals 10, 16
diamonds 52
dinosaurs 29, 34–35, 41, 53
erosion 20–21
fossil-hunting 42–43
fossil plants 36–37, 38
fuels 38–39
gneiss 18
granite 7, 11, 18
igneous rocks 8, 9, 52
lava 8, 9
limestone 12, 14, 16, 53
magma 9
marble 16, 17, 27, 52
Mauna Loa 52
metamorphic rocks 16–17
meteorites 24–25, 53
minerals 6, 7, 10, 15, 53
palaeontologists 29, 42

pyramids 53
sandstone 15
schist 19
sedimentary rocks 12–15, 27
shells 12, 28
slate 19
starfish 33
Taj Mahal 52
tektites 25
trilobites 28, 32
volcanoes 8, 52, 53
weathering 20–21, 22–23

Rocks and fossils
quiz answers

1) C   7) C
2) B   8) B
3) B   9) A
4) A   10) A
5) C   11) B
6) A   12) A